Tell Me Why

FOOD
Questions and Answers

by
Rebecca Phillips-Bartlett

BEARPORT
PUBLISHING

Minneapolis, Minnesota

Credits
All images are courtesy of Shutterstock.com, unless otherwise specified. With thanks to Getty Images, Thinkstock Photo, and iStockphoto.

Cover – GoodStudio, ivector. Throughout– Perfectorius, Orgus88, Natalia Sheinkin, Ali Designer 20, Nattapol_Sritongcom, BNP Design Studio, Aliva. 4–5 – subkontr, RinArte, Prihanto Edi, Andrey Elkin, nantonov, xamtiw, MD MAHADI HASAN RABBI. 6–7 – Alejo Miranda, Macrovector, Sira Anamwong, Angyee Patipat, BATKA, Vasilyeva Larisa, pinkpeachberry, WinWin artlab, Assja. 8–9 – Lemberg Vector studio, Colorfuel Studio, MrslePew, lemono, hanapon1002. 10–11 – Colorfuel Studio, Lana Nikova, huntingSHARK. 12–13 – Nicoleta Ionescu, lemono, Elena Pimukova, Maxim Goulidow, Picsfive, buyit, vencavolrab, AaronAmat. 14–15 – Olena Dumanchuk, MicroOne, rimglow, valentinarr. 16–17 – Vectorbum, BNP Design Studio, BeataGFX, t_kimura. 18–19 – AlexanderTrou, Anydudl, HappyPictures, GreenSkyStudio, RinArte, only_fabrizio, juliannafunk. 20–21 – Iconic Bestiary, WinWin artlab, Camillea, xpixel, Jamakosy, SvetlanaK, ThamKC. 22–23 – BeataGFX, Lena_Zajchikova, artphotoclub, Gizelka, Afonkin_Yuriy.

Bearport Publishing Company Product Development Team
Publisher: Jen Jenson; Director of Product Development: Spencer Brinker; Managing Editor: Allison Juda; Editor: Cole Nelson; Associate Editor: Naomi Reich; Associate Editor: Tiana Tran; Art Director: Colin O'Dea; Designer: Kim Jones; Designer: Kayla Eggert; Product Development Specialist: Owen Hamlin

Library of Congress Cataloging-in-Publication Data is available at www.loc.gov or upon request from the publisher.

ISBN: 979-8-89232-755-8 (hardcover)
ISBN: 979-8-89232-951-4 (paperback)
ISBN: 979-8-89232-842-5 (ebook)

© 2025 BookLife Publishing
This edition is published by arrangement with BookLife Publishing.

North American adaptations © 2025 Bearport Publishing Company. All rights reserved. No part of this publication may be reproduced in whole or in part, stored in any retrieval system, or transmitted in any form or by any means, electronic, mechanical, photocopying, recording, or otherwise, without written permission from the publisher.

For more information, write to Bearport Publishing, 5357 Penn Avenue South, Minneapolis, MN 55419.

Contents

Tell Me Why 4

Why Do Foods Have Different Tastes? 6

Why Do People Eat Different Kinds of Food around the World? 7

Why Do Sour Foods Make My Face Scrunch Up? 8

Why Do Spicy Foods Make My Nose Run? .10

Why Does Cutting Onions Make Me Cry? 11

Why Do People Have Allergic Reactions? 12

Why Are Fruits and Vegetables Good for Me? 14

Why Do the Same Fruits Sometimes Taste Different? 15

Why Does Food Taste Different When I Have a Stuffy Nose? 16

Why Do We Refrigerate Food? 18

Why Do Some Kinds of Cheese Stink? 19

Why Does Popcorn Pop? 20

Why Do Cakes Rise? 21

Asking Questions 22

Glossary 24

Index 24

TELL ME WHY

All animals need food. That includes humans. Luckily for us, there are many kinds of foods all around the world.

QUESTION
What questions do you have about food?

Food is part of our daily lives, but it can still be surprising. Some foods have strange tastes and smells. Sometimes, food makes our bodies do odd things. There are so many things about food that leave us wondering **WHY?**

WHY DO FOODS HAVE DIFFERENT TASTES?

There are five basic tastes. They are salty, sweet, sour, **umami** (oo-MAH-mee), and bitter. These tastes are caused by different **chemicals** in food.

Sugars, salts, and **acids** are some of the chemicals that cause taste. As you eat, taste buds on your tongue sense these things. Then, they send messages to your brain to identify the taste.

FUN FACT
Your taste buds change over time, so you may like different foods as you get older.

WHY DO PEOPLE EAT DIFFERENT KINDS OF FOOD AROUND THE WORLD?

Plants make up a big part of what people eat. However, different plants grow best with different kinds of weather. People often eat things that grow well in their part of the world.

Food is a part of **culture**, too. Many places have dishes that are important to the people who live there.

WHY DO SOUR FOODS MAKE MY FACE SCRUNCH UP?

Sour foods have acids in them. When your taste buds sense acid, they cause your face to scrunch up. This is called a **rejection** response.

In the past, people had to gather their food from nature. The rejection response helped them decide which foods could be harmful.

Today, most people get food from the store, but the rejection response is still useful. Some foods start to taste sour when they go bad. This tells you not to eat them.

WHY DO SPICY FOODS MAKE MY NOSE RUN?

The burning feeling from spicy food is usually caused by a chemical in chili peppers called capsaicin (kap-SAY-uh-sin). This chemical is an **irritant**. Your body makes lots of **mucus** to try and get rid of the irritant. Eventually, some of the mucus runs out of your nose as snot.

FUN FACT

Capsaicin stops hungry animals from eating chili peppers. However, many humans enjoy the spicy feeling.

WHY DOES CUTTING ONIONS MAKE ME CRY?

Onions release an irritating gas when their skin is broken. They do this to stop hungry animals from eating them. When you cut into an onion, the gas floats into the air around you. Your eyes create tears to try to wash the irritant away.

WHY DO PEOPLE HAVE ALLERGIC REACTIONS?

People have allergic **reactions** because their bodies mistakenly think things that are normally safe can cause harm. The strong reactions are the bodies trying to protect themselves.

Some people have allergic reactions to food. Even though the food itself is fine, the reaction can be very harmful. It can cause a rash, stomach pain, swelling, and other uncomfortable effects.

FUN FACT

Things that cause allergic reactions are called allergens. Nuts, milk, and eggs are common allergens.

WHY ARE FRUITS AND VEGETABLES GOOD FOR ME?

Your body needs **nutrients** to stay healthy. Fruits and veggies are full of many different nutrients. Eating these foods helps your body grow and stay strong.

Fruits and vegetables also have lots of fiber. Fiber helps your body **digest** the food you eat.

QUESTION
Which are your favorite fruits and veggies to eat?

WHY DO THE SAME FRUITS SOMETIMES TASTE DIFFERENT?

Fruits grow on plants. Changes in the weather, soil, and amount of sunlight plants get can affect how their fruits taste.

Fruits also taste best when they are perfectly ripe. If fruits are picked too soon or too late, they probably won't taste as good.

WHY DOES FOOD TASTE DIFFERENT WHEN I HAVE A STUFFY NOSE?

When you are sick, foods may seem to have a different flavor.

Having a cold does not change the actual taste of food. However, a stuffy nose can limit the flavors you're able to sense.

Flavor is the way your brain understands taste. It is a combination of your senses of taste and smell. When your nose is stuffy, you might not be able to smell as well. So, the flavor might seem different.

FUN FACT
People often plug their noses when they eat or drink something that tastes bad, such as medicine.

WHY DO WE REFRIGERATE FOOD?

Some foods go bad faster if they are not kept cold. This is because the bacteria on these foods grow fastest when it is warm. Keeping food in a cold fridge means bacteria grow more slowly. This keeps food safer for longer.

FUN FACT
Food often has some bacteria. However, too much of some kinds can make people sick.

WHY DO SOME KINDS OF CHEESE STINK?

Cheese is made from milk that has been separated into lumps and liquid. The lumps are pressed into a solid block of cheese. Some blocks are specially washed and aged to give them a coating called a rind. The stink comes from bacteria that grow on the rind.

WHY DOES POPCORN POP?

Popcorn starts as a hard seed called a kernel. Inside each kernel is **starch** and water. As the kernel heats up, the water **expands**. The water takes up more and more space until . . . *Pop!* The starch pushes outward and turns the kernel into a fluffy piece of popcorn.

WHY DO CAKES RISE?

Baking involves lots of chemical changes. The ingredients in some foods can cause all kinds of reactions.

Many cakes contain baking soda or baking powder. When these things mix with liquid in a batter, they create small gas bubbles. As the gas bubbles are heated, they grow larger. This makes cakes rise.

FUN FACT
When you put a cake in the oven, you are starting a chemical reaction.

Asking Questions

This book is full of questions you might have had about food. How do we know the answers? Because many people before you have asked the same things.

Asking questions is a great way to learn about the world around you. There are still so many interesting things to discover about food. So, stay curious, and keep asking questions!

QUESTION

What other questions do you have about food?

Glossary

acids chemicals that can break things down

chemicals natural or human-made substances that can sometimes be harmful

culture the traditions, ideas, and ways of life of a group of people

digest to break down food into things that can be used by the body

expands grows bigger and takes up more space

irritant something that causes discomfort

mucus a slimy substance, such as snot, found in parts of the body

nutrients substances in food needed by living things to grow and stay healthy

reactions responses to things that happen

rejection the action of refusing or getting rid of something

starch a substance found in foods such as potatoes

umami a rich taste found in some foods

Index

bacteria 18–19
chemicals 6, 10, 21
culture 7
flavor 16–17
fridge 18
fruit 14–15
mucus 10
reaction 12–13, 21
response 8–9
smell 5, 17
taste buds 6, 8
water 20
weather 7, 15